AF599411

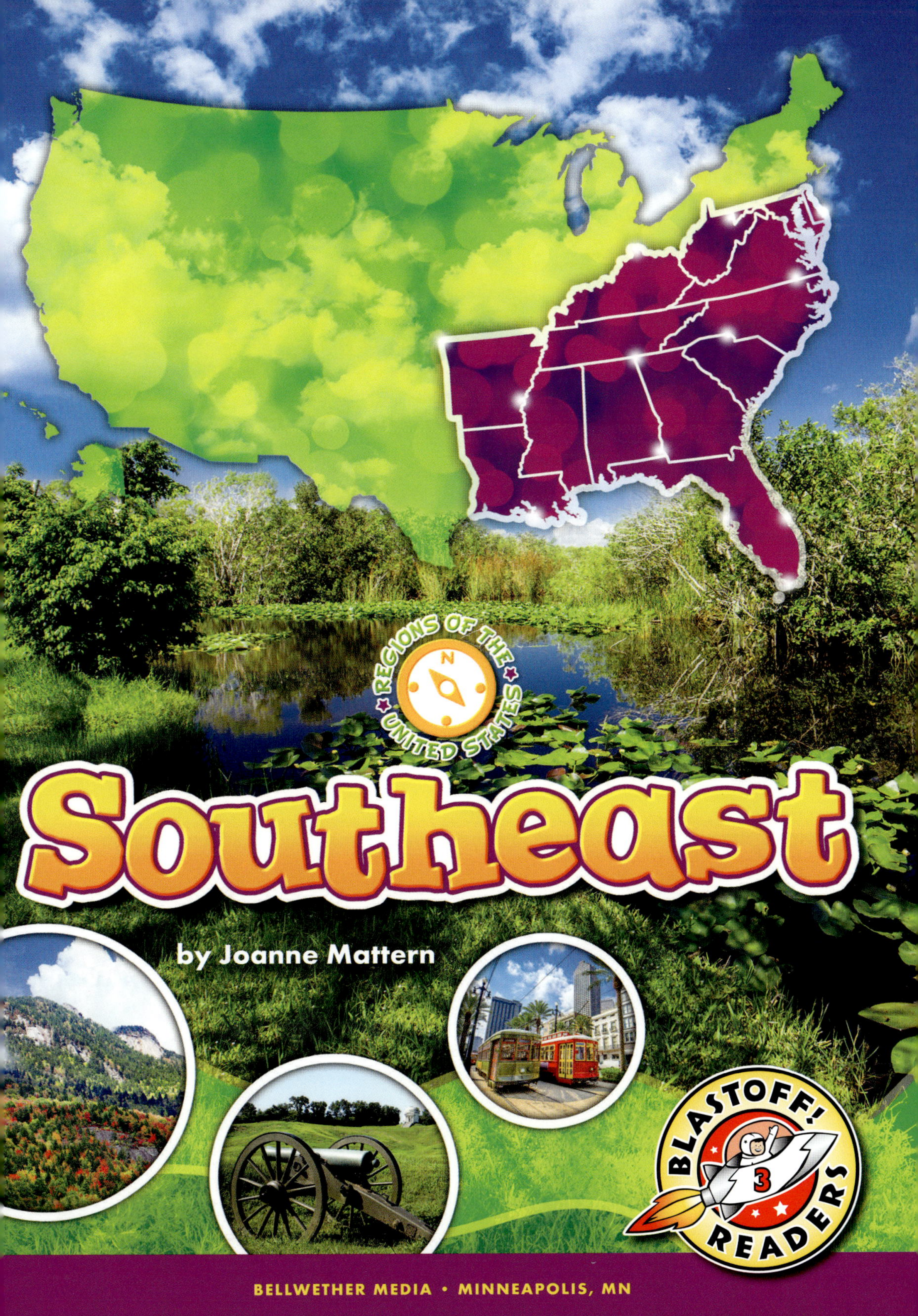
Regions of the United States
N
Southeast
by Joanne Mattern
Blastoff! Readers
3
Bellwether Media • Minneapolis, MN

Blastoff! Readers are carefully developed by literacy experts to build reading stamina and move students toward fluency by combining standards-based content with developmentally appropriate text.

Level 1 provides the most support through repetition of high-frequency words, light text, predictable sentence patterns, and strong visual support.

Level 2 offers early readers a bit more challenge through varied sentences, increased text load, and text-supportive special features.

Level 3 advances early-fluent readers toward fluency through increased text load, less reliance on photos, advancing concepts, longer sentences, and more complex special features.

★ **Blastoff! Universe**

Reading Level

Grade K

Grades 1–3

Grade 4

This edition first published in 2025 by Bellwether Media, Inc.

Library of Congress Cataloging-in-Publication Data

Names: Mattern, Joanne, 1963- author.
Title: Southeast / Joanne Mattern.
Description: Minneapolis, MN : Bellwether Media, Inc., 2025. | Series: Blastoff! readers: Regions of the United States | Includes bibliographical references and index. | Audience: Ages 5-8 | Audience: Grades 2-3 | Summary: "Simple text and full-color photography introduce beginning readers to the Southeast. Developed by literacy experts for students in kindergarten through third grade"-Provided by publisher.
Identifiers: LCCN 2024039183 (print) | LCCN 2024039184 (ebook) | ISBN 9798893042498 (library binding) | ISBN 9798893043464 (ebook)
Subjects: LCSH: Southern States--Juvenile literature.
Classification: LCC F209.3 .M3882025 (print) | LCC F209.3 (ebook) | DDC 975--dc23/eng/20240910
LC record available at https://lccn.loc.gov/2024039183
LC ebook record available at https://lccn.loc.gov/2024039184

Editor: Kieran Downs Designer: Brittany McIntosh

Printed in the United States of America, North Mankato, MN.

Table of Contents

Welcome to the Southeast!

The Southeast is a region of the United States. The region includes 14 states and 1 **district**.

The Southeast is home to many beautiful places. It was also the center of the **civil rights** movement.

States in the Southeast

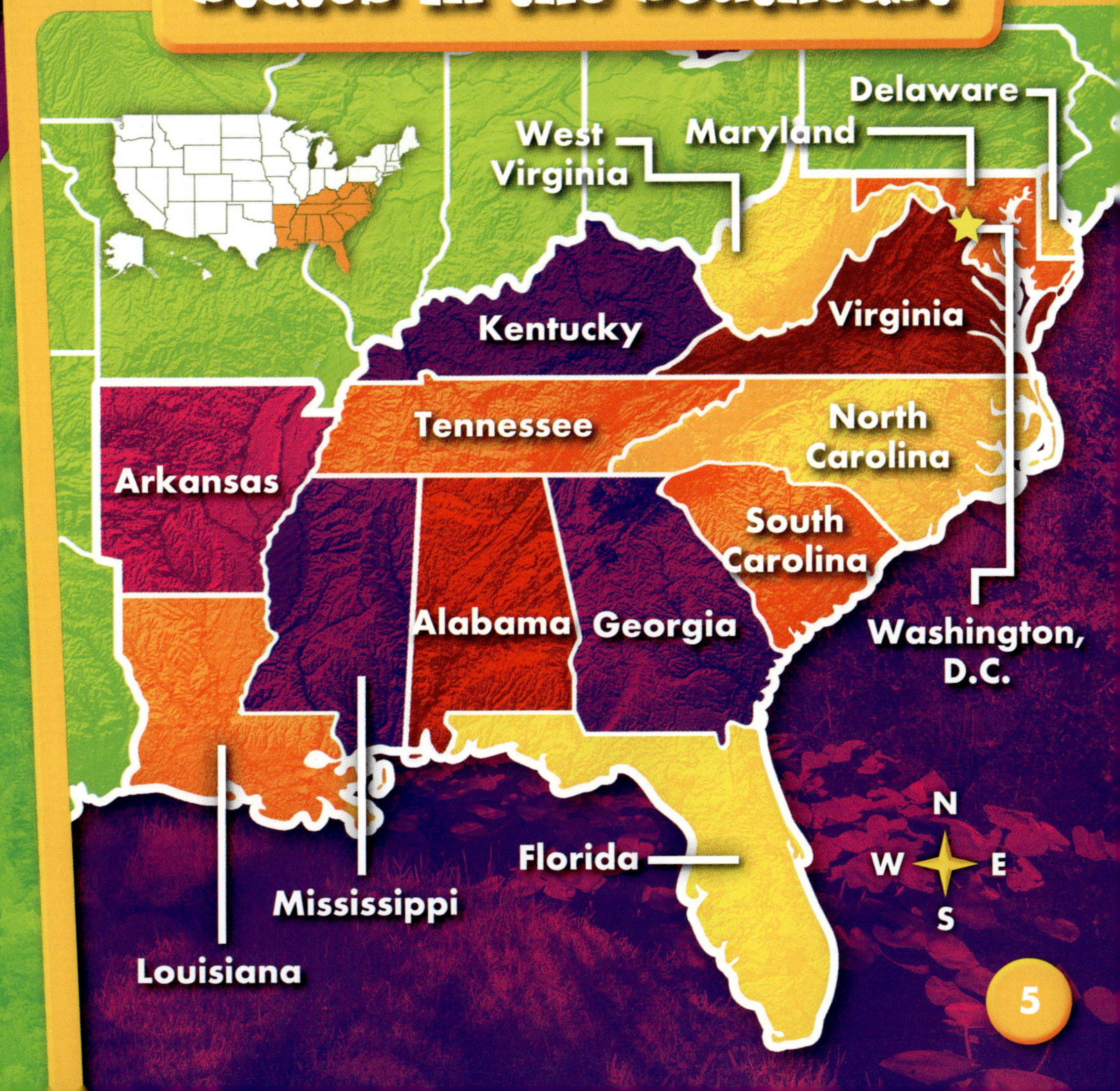

Delaware
West Virginia
Maryland
Kentucky
Virginia
Tennessee
North Carolina
Arkansas
South Carolina
Alabama
Georgia
Washington, D.C.
Florida
Mississippi
Louisiana
N
W
E
S

The Land, Weather, and Wildlife

Great Smoky Mountains

The Appalachian Mountains run through the Southeast. These include the Blue Ridge and Great Smoky Mountains.

There are many **wetlands** in the Southeast. Coastal areas lie along the Atlantic Ocean and the **Gulf** of Mexico.

hurricane

Most of the Southeast has a **subtropical** climate. It is often hot and **humid**. Winters are mild with some rain.

Hurricanes often strike in the summer and fall. These powerful storms can cause a lot of damage.

National Mall

Location

Washington, D.C.

Famous For

Many museums, statues, and monuments

The Southeast is home to many animals. Foxes and black bears live in the forests.

fox

Many birds live near the ocean. They include spoonbills and pelicans. Turtles and alligators swim in swamps and lakes.

Natural Resources and Industry

Agriculture is important in the Southeast. The warm, wet weather makes for long growing seasons. Farmers raise many crops.

Many ships travel in and out of harbors along the coast. Factories build airplanes, rockets, and other aircraft.

People of the Southeast

Many people in the Southeast have European **ancestry**. Others have African ancestors. Many are the **descendants** of **enslaved** people.

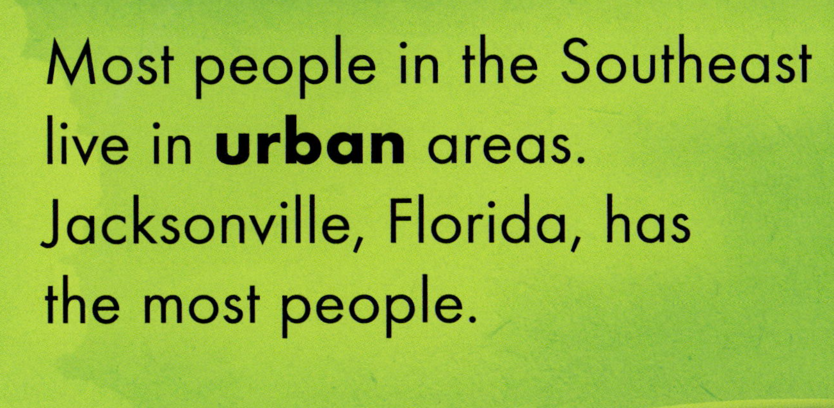

Most people in the Southeast live in **urban** areas. Jacksonville, Florida, has the most people.

Jacksonville, Florida

Food is an important part of life in the Southeast. The area is known for its fish and seafood dishes.

Spicy Cajun food began in Louisiana. People in the Southeast also enjoy different kinds of **barbecue**.

Music is a big part of life in the Southeast. People come together for music festivals.

People enjoy being outdoors. They swim in the ocean. They hike in the mountains and forests. The Southeast is a beautiful place!

music festival

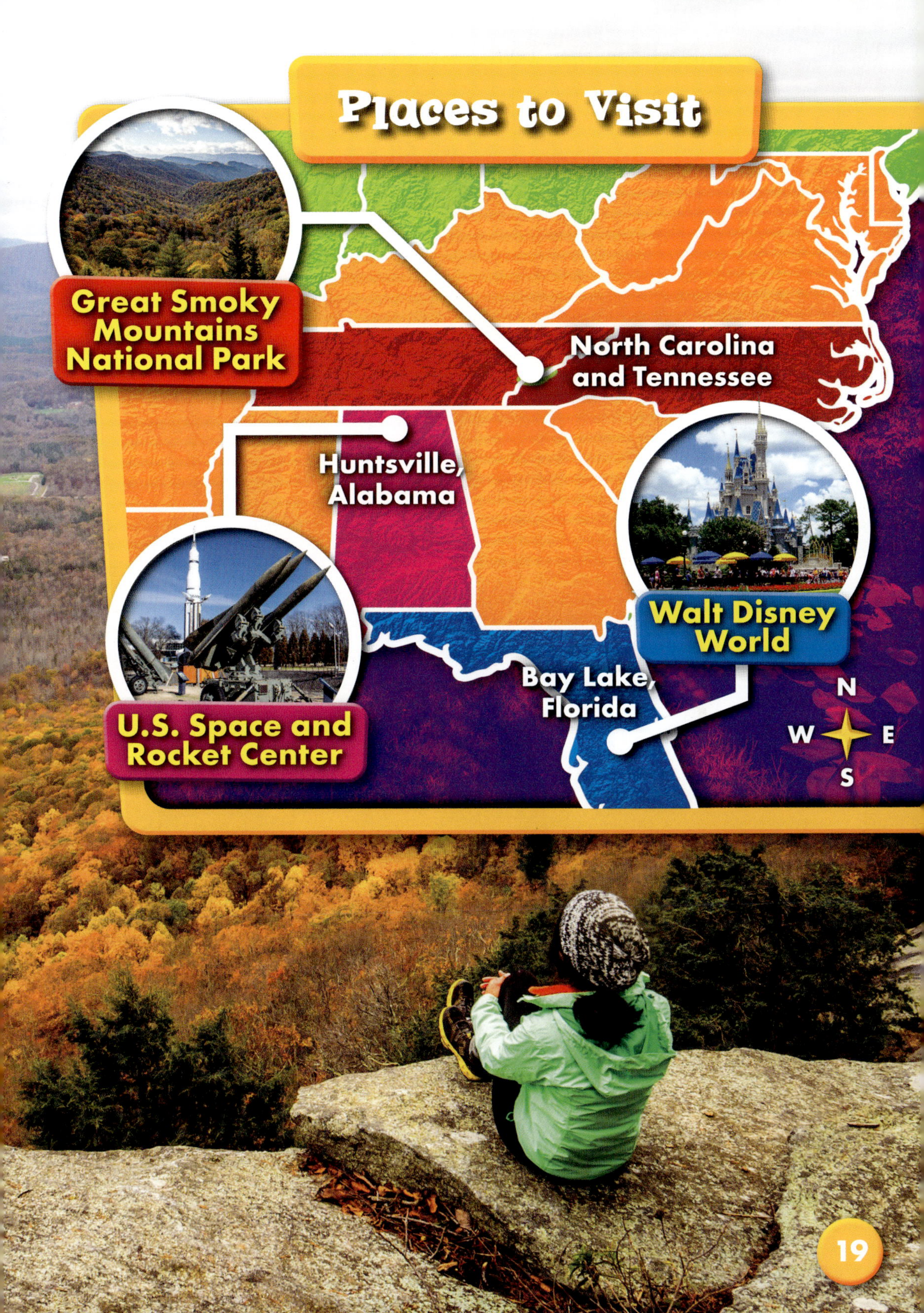
Places to Visit
Great Smoky Mountains National Park
North Carolina and Tennessee
Huntsville, Alabama
Walt Disney World
Bay Lake, Florida
U.S. Space and Rocket Center
N
W
E
S

Southeast Fast Facts

3 Largest Cities (2020)

1

Jacksonville, Florida

Population:
949,611

2

Charlotte, North Carolina

Population:
874,579

3

Washington, D.C.

Population:
689,545

State Populations (2020)

Washington, D.C.
689,545

Delaware
989,948

Maryland
6.2 million

Virginia
8.6 million

North Carolina
10.4 million

South Carolina
5.1 million

Georgia
10.7 million

Florida
21.5 million

Alabama
5 million

Mississippi
3 million

Louisiana
4.7 million

Arkansas
3 million

Tennessee
6.9 million

Kentucky
4.5 million

West Virginia
1.8 million

Major Sports Teams

Baltimore Orioles
(MLB)

Washington Commanders
(NFL)

Miami Heat
(NBA)

Famous Face

Name: Martin Luther King, Jr.
Hometown: Atlanta, Georgia
Famous for: Civil rights leader

Smallest State

Delaware
2,489 square miles
(6,446 square kilometers)

Largest State

Florida
65,758 square miles
(170,312 square kilometers)

Glossary

agriculture—the practice of raising crops and animals

ancestry—a person's ancestors; ancestors are relatives who lived a long time ago.

barbecue—food that is seasoned and slowly cooked over an open fire

civil rights—the rights all people have to freedom and equal treatment under the law

descendants—people related to a person or group of people who lived at an earlier time

district—an area or region

enslaved—to be considered property and forced to work for no pay

gulf—a part of an ocean or sea extending into land

humid—having a lot of water in the air

hurricanes—large, powerful storms that begin over the ocean and can move onto land

subtropical—referring to a climate that has hot, humid summers and mild winters

urban—related to cities or city life

wetlands—areas of land that are covered with low levels of water for most of the year

To Learn More

AT THE LIBRARY

Sebra, Richard. *Washington, DC.* Minneapolis, Minn.: Abdo Publishing, 2023.

Sexton, Colleen. *Florida.* Minneapolis, Minn.: Bellwether Media, 2022.

Spanier, Kristine. *Explore the South.* Minneapolis, Minn.: Jump!, 2023.

ON THE WEB

FACTSURFER

Factsurfer.com gives you a safe, fun way to find more information.

1. Go to www.factsurfer.com.
2. Enter "Southeast" into the search box and click 🔍.
3. Select your book cover to see a list of related content.

Index

The images in this book are reproduced through the courtesy of: Mia2you, front cover (main), p. 8; Steve Bower, front cover (bottom left); Suzanne C. Grim, front cover (bottom center); Sean Pavone, front cover (bottom right), p. 19 (Great Smoky Mountains National Park); Svetlana Foote, p. 3; Stacy Funderburke, p. 4; Jeff Morgan, p. 6; Bill_Richardson, p. 7 (top); Cvandyke, p. 7 (bottom); Kamira, p. 9; Sandra Standbridge, p. 10; kpkellyfl, p. 11 (top); deannalindsey, p. 11 (bottom); Daniel Wright98, p. 12; Mccallk69, p. 13 (right); Kosoff, p. 14; ESB Professional, p. 15; Brent Hofacker, p. 16; Sokor Space, p. 17 (top); Teri Virbickis, p. 17 (bottom); Liz Mangels, p. 18; Panpilas L, pp. 18-19; Sunshine/ Alamy Stock Photo, p. 19 (Walt Disney World); Danny Ye, p. 19 (U.S. Space and Rocket Center); Paul Brennan, p. 20 (Jacksonville); Kevin Ruck, p. 20 (Charlotte); lunamrina, p. 20 (Washington, D.C.); Baltimore Orioles/ Wikipedia, p. 21 (Orioles logo); Washington Commanders/ Wikipedia, p. 21 (Commanders logo); Miami Heat/ Wikipedia, p. 21 (Heat logo); IanDagnall Computing/ Alamy, p. 21 (Martin Luther King Jr.); Eric Isselee, p. 23.